Decorative

MARBLING

Decorative MARBLING

SOLVEIG STONE

MEREHURST

For Humphrey, Angelica, Emily, Lucy and Clementine

Published in 1993 by Merehurst Limited, Ferry House
51–57 Lacy Road, Putney, London SW15 1PR

Copyright © Merehurst Limited 1993

ISBN 1–85391–299–9

A catalogue record of this book is available from the British Library.

Edited by **Miren Lopategui**
Designed by **Lisa Tai**
Photography by **Di Lewis** (pages 4, 7, 22–5 and 64–7);
all other photography by **Jon Bouchier**
Illustrations by **Paul Dewhurst**

NB: *In this book the terms 'cellulose size' and*
'courlose powder size' are interchangeable.

Typeset by J&L Composition Ltd
Colour separation by Global Colour
Printed in Italy

Contents

Introduction

A BRIEF HISTORY OF MARBLING

Marbling is an ancient craft which remained cloaked in mystery until this century. The oldest form of marbling on paper began in 12th-century Japan. Known as *suminagashi*, which literally means 'floating ink', the art was handed from one generation to the next by a custom of teaching the process to only one child in a family. For several hundred years, the use of marbled paper was restricted to the royal household only.

The earliest documented sheet of marbled paper, known as Ebru, dates from the 15th century and came from the Near East. It was here that glue was first added to water to form size. This gave marblers much more control over their colours, and formed the basis of today's marbling techniques. Little is known of its early history, however, except that, according to tradition, it travelled along the silk routes and first appeared in Europe in the mid-sixteenth century, where it became enormously treasured by collectors. Early marblers are believed to have come to Italy, set up shop and taught the Italians the craft. From there it soon travelled to France, Germany and the Netherlands.

In England, marbling as a craft grew more slowly, and only became an important industry in the nineteenth century, when the first book to explain marbling techniques appeared. Published by Woolnough in 1853, it caused consternation that hitherto well-kept secrets had finally been given away. Up till then, masters had kept their secrets by never teaching the whole process to any one apprentice. Young boys were selected from the local workhouse, and one would be taught how to prepare colours, another to polish paper, while yet another would be taught how to create a few patterns. In this century, the craft was kept alive virtually single-handedly in England by the binders and marblers Cockerell and Sons.

Since the 1970s, marbling has found a new popularity. It is no longer used only by bookbinders but has acquired new devotees among designers and manufacturers,

An ancient craft with a contemporary appeal, marbling has adapted perfectly to a wide range of modern uses.

who have come to appreciate the many uses marbling designs may be put to. I now regularly produce special designs for an amazing variety of uses – from borders to greeting cards to packaging for supermarket tissue boxes, and even packaging for condoms!

The fascination of transferring floating inks or paints on to paper appeals to all ages, however. There is a kind of magic in the process. Marbling allows great freedom of expression with colour and it is impossible not to achieve immediate results. My own impatient nature was attracted to marbling for exactly this reason.

THE STORY OF COMPTON MARBLING

My own interest in marbling began over 20 years ago, when I went to California as a young bride. My husband, Humphrey, had been appointed art director of the Stanford University Press, and we were living in northern California. While waiting for a work permit, I used to spend hours exploring the university campus and in the library there I came across a superb collection of bindings by Cobden-Sanderson – Victorian contemporaries of William Morris. I was instantly captivated by the stunning marbled endpapers, and became obsessed with learning how to marble – despite the fact

that I had had no form of art school education whatsoever. (I am convinced that this accessibility to everyone is the key to marbling's attraction.)

I had to wait for a few years, however, until we returned to England and found ourselves living in Wiltshire, before I could embark on the process of learning. Trial and error is the only way. Paints are notoriously temperamental and tricky – the pigments have an infuriating habit of reacting against one another – and I also had to learn the importance of temperature. I was extremely fortunate, however, in having a husband with a razor-sharp eye. He had, by now, joined the printers The Compton Press, where, to my undying amazement, there was a marbling room. I persevered in my efforts because of Humphrey's superhuman support – and deadlines for marbled paper from The Compton Press. (There is nothing like the pressure of a deadline!) It was years, however, before I could walk into the marbling room and know that I was in control of the paints. But oddly enough, despite all the difficulties, it was still totally compulsive, and, although extremely frustrating at times, it was always difficult to stop for the day.

In 1973, I paused briefly to have our first daughter, Angelica, followed two years later by Emily. By then I had quite decided that I should have to give up marbling. How could I possibly look after a family, run a house *and* meet deadlines? Six weeks later, I was back at the tank and the routine continued. I marbled when the children slept and in the summer they played outside my window while I worked.

The turning point for me came when Emily had just learnt to stand. I can't remember who first had the idea, but Caroline Mann, whose husband had by then joined the Compton Press, began to marble with me. This vastly increased our output. When I finished a shift in the shed she began, and we continued like this until she had her first baby – and the same need as me to have a 'marbling shed' in her own garden.

In 1979, we were selected for the first ever Chelsea Crafts Fair. By then we were producing approximately 20,000 sheets of marbled paper per year, and we started to use the paper to cover our own range of products. Now our colour catalogue contains over 70 products, ranging from candle-shades to CD boxes – all covered with marbled papers. These days, trade fairs periodically take me away from the marbling tank, and exports make up a sizeable part of the turnover. Things have moved on a great deal. At first I had to keep a recipe book for each pattern, carefully recording the order in which the paints were applied, and which paints made up each colour. Now, although I am constantly producing new patterns, and have recently added gold, bronze and silver to my range, my years of experience and practice help me to tell at a glance how each colour is arrived at. Marbling has always given me an enormous amount of enjoyment. I very much hope you will find this guide a help, and that you will have as much pleasure as I have in experimenting with different paints and patterns.

Equipment and Materials

Marbling is an ideal craft for beginners because most of the equipment needed is readily available and cheap. And because there are no rigid rules, many of the items you need can be easily adapted from things around the house. The equipment shown here is for use with oil paints. Materials for marbling with water-based paints are shown on page 13.

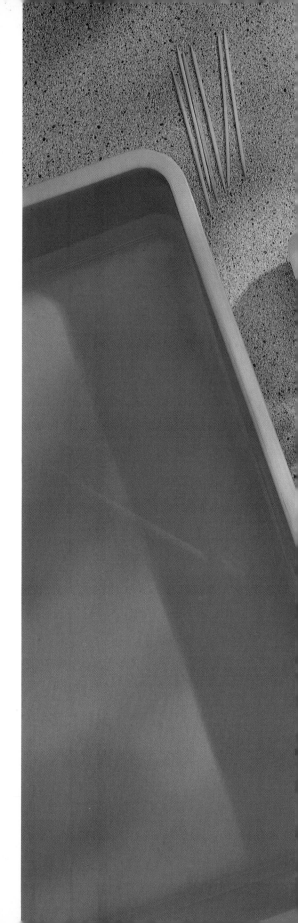

Equipment and materials

MARBLING IS A MARVELLOUS MEANS OF SELF-expression. It is also, unfortunately, rather messy, so your first important consideration will be to find somewhere to do it. You will need a table with enough space for your pots of paint and brushes – and, preferably, a large free area around it. I also always recommend sheets of plastic to protect the floor, and, if there's a wall in front of the table, a covering for that too. The paint flies everywhere!

For the best results, you will also need the right atmospheric conditions. Marbling, alas, is not synonymous with comfort and the ideal conditions are slightly damp, cool and dust-free. A garden shed is perfect! Access to fresh air is vital to avoid the fumes from the white spirit you will be using to thin the paint. If using water-based paints, you must also have a sink or outside tap at hand for rinsing your marbled paper.

Once you have established all these requirements, you can then concentrate on more specific equipment. Below are all the basics you will need for oil and water marbling. Bear in mind that you will need additional combs as you start to experiment with more complicated patterns.

ALUM

Alum solution is sponged over all paper that is marbled with water-based paints, to make the paper absorb the paints properly. You will not need it when working with oil paints. (Don't forget: you will also need a sponge to apply the solution, and rubber gloves to protect your hands.)

Key Diagram

1 Marbling tank
2 Cocktail sticks (to use as a stylus)
3 Ox gall
4 White spirit
5 Panel pins and comb
6 Pots for mixing paints
7 Paints
8 Paintbrushes
9 Paste powder
10 Selection of papers

BRUSHES, EYEDROPPERS AND POTS

Brushes are generally only used with oil paints. Almost any bristle paintbrush from a hardware shop or decorating suppliers will do. Brushes are measured by the width of the bristle, and the ones most often used in marbling measure 6mm (¼in), 12mm (½in) and 2.5cm (1in), though the wider 2.5cm (1in) brush will generally only be used for applying background colour. The width and length of bristles are important if you are to control your paint properly. Children's paintbrushes, for example, are very well suited to marbling, but you may have to cut the bristles if they are too long, to stop the paint from flying about. Similarly, brushes that are too chunky will take up too much paint, which will cause problems when trying to control the amount of paint landing on the paper.

Eyedroppers are used instead of brushes when working with watercolours. They are not suitable for oil paints because they are too difficult to clean.

Pots are used for mixing the paints. Anything such as a jam jar or coffee tin will do, as long as it is wide enough to mix your paints easily. Yogurt pots are useful because they are disposable, but they are also very light, so watch out that your brush doesn't tip the pot over.

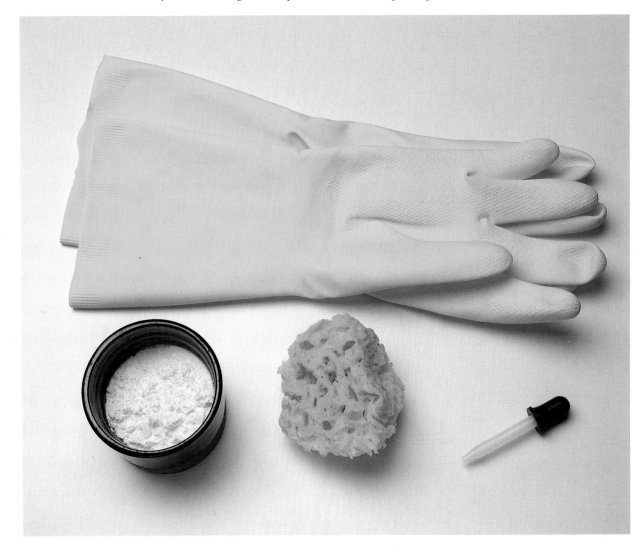

The four items illustrated here – alum, eyedropper, sponge and rubber gloves – are used only for marbling with watercolours. They are not needed at all for oil paints.

COMBS

Combs are used to create specific patterns, which will vary according to the width between the teeth in the comb. (The narrower the teeth, the more intricate the pattern.) A hair comb with long teeth – the type used for permed hair – can achieve quite effective results, but the best option is to make your own.

One simple way of doing this is to bang panel pins through a piece of thin (about 12mm (½in) thick) plywood which measures either the length or width of your marbling tank. For a first attempt, panel pins set 12mm (½in) apart will give an easy

comb to make and use. It may be easier to use if you attach a knob handle on top.

An alternative method is to stick long dressmaker's pins into a narrow piece of balsa wood – the sharp end into the wood. This is the quickest way of all to make a marbling comb, but be warned: if you use the comb a great deal, the paint will eventually build up on the pin heads.

A third, inexpensive, way of making a comb is described and illustrated below. Like the other two versions, it has pins set 12mm (½in) apart – the most suitable width for a beginner. As you progress you will need two further combs – one with pins

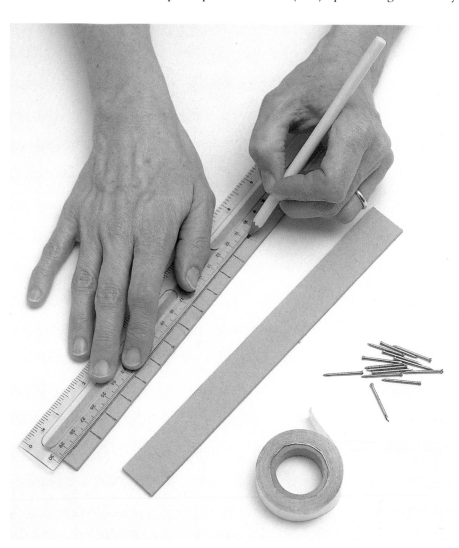

1
MAKING A COMB
Cut two pieces of cardboard about 7.5cm (3in) deep by the length you require. Attach double-sided tape to one of the pieces.

2
Distribute the pins 12mm (½in) apart and lay them on double-sided tape so that they will not move.

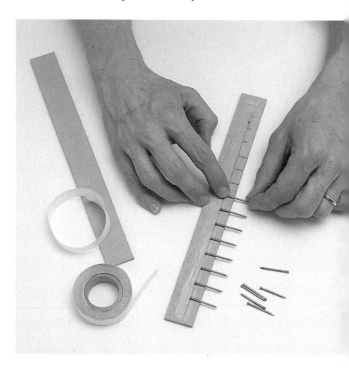

set 6mm (¼in) apart and another with pins set 3mm (⅛in) apart (see Experimenting with Patterns, page 30).

DRYING RACK

All marbled sheets need to be left to dry. A concertina clothes drying rack is perfect, or you can make up a line of string with clothes pegs and peg the paper on that. Alternatively, you could have a plastic sheet or newspaper to lay the marbled sheets on. It really depends on how much space you have and how many sheets of paper you marble at a time.

MARBLING TANK

This is where you will actually create your patterns and lay your paper on the surface of the size, so you need to bear the following factors in mind. The tank should, ideally, be flat-bottomed, and about 5cm (2in) deep. It can be slightly deeper than this, but not too much or you may find it difficult to lay the paper evenly on the surface. It should also be at least 2.5cm (1in) larger all round than the paper you want to marble, to allow enough room for your fingers to lay the paper down.

Marbling tanks can be made from a variety of materials, such as metal or watertight plastic. You

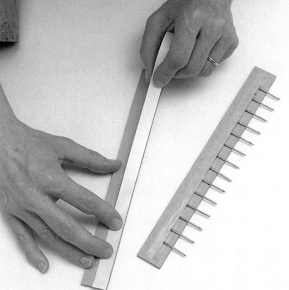

3
Lay another strip of double-sided tape on to the second piece of cardboard and press down firmly to secure.

4
Press the two pieces of cardboard firmly together to complete the final stage of the comb.

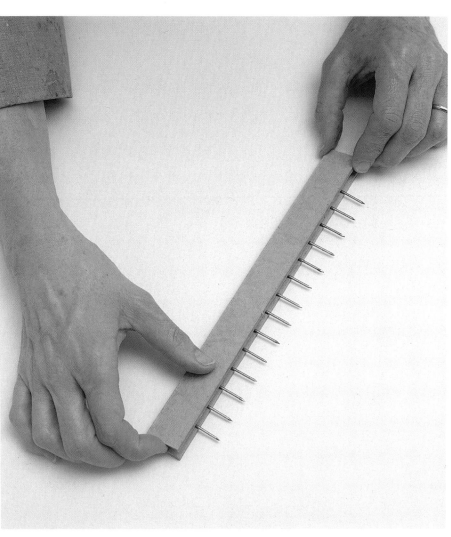

can even make your own, using heavy-duty plastic (the type used for lining ponds) nailed to strips of wood, although once you become experienced you may prefer to have one tailor-made for you by a blacksmith. If you're a beginner, however, a cat litter tray is probably the cheapest and most accessible option although once you start using large sheets of paper, you will have to progress to something bigger.

Bear in mind that your tank will need to be continually emptied, so if you do decide to have one made, it should have a draining tap at one end. A tank full of size is heavy so bear this in mind when you plan where you are going to marble. You will either need to empty the tank into a bucket or carry it to a suitable drain.

PAINTS, THINNERS AND OX GALL

Paints for marbling can be either oil- or water-based. My own particular preference is for oil paints – either artist's or student's oils, though the latter are cheaper. Whichever you choose, thin them with white spirit, not turpentine which will be too oily. Any water-based paints such as poster paints can be used, though these will, of course, be thinned with water.

Ox gall is the vital ingredient for any marbler, whichever type of paint you are using, to reduce the surface tension on the water or size, and to help the paints disperse properly on the surface of the tank. You can also try washing up liquid – it is certainly cheaper – although you may need to experiment with amounts a little at first.

Plain brown paper is perfect for experimenting with as a beginner, but as your marbling skills improve you can progress to other types of paper. Tinted papers, ranging from pale to dark colours, offer particularly interesting effects. The same paint can change dramatically when applied on to the different shades.

PAPER

The best paper to use for marbling is uncoated paper – that is, any paper which does not have a very shiny surface. If the paper is too slippery, the paints won't be absorbed. If it is too thin, it will tear when wet. A good example is tissue paper, which looks very pretty when marbled, but will disintegrate if it absorbs too much water.

Any type of fairly strong, absorbent paper is ideal. Plain brown, or kraft, paper is perfect for experimenting because it is so cheap. The same applies to copy paper, which is another cheap alternative. You can always progress to more expensive bond or laid paper later, as you become more skilled.

Tinted or textured papers can produce very interesting effects. Used with gold and silver paints, they can make attractive and unusual giftwrapping paper (see pages 42–43).

PAPER STRIPS

You will need strips of newspaper or any other absorbent paper to clean the surface of the tank after marbling each sheet. They should, ideally, measure 5–7.5cm (2–3in) wide by the length of the marbling tank you are using.

SIZE

Size is a mixture of water and gelatine, and is used to hold the pattern. It can be made from Courlose powder, or, more commonly, carragheen moss (Irish seaweed). Non-fungicide wallpaper paste, if you can find it, is also acceptable.

STYLUS

Styluses are used to create a swirl or feather pattern. They are also used in the first step of all combed patterns. The basic requirement for any stylus is that it should be fairly thin and easy to pick up. If you don't have a stylus, there are many things you can use instead, such as darning needles, cocktail sticks, or any long wire rod. My own particular preference is for thin knitting needles.

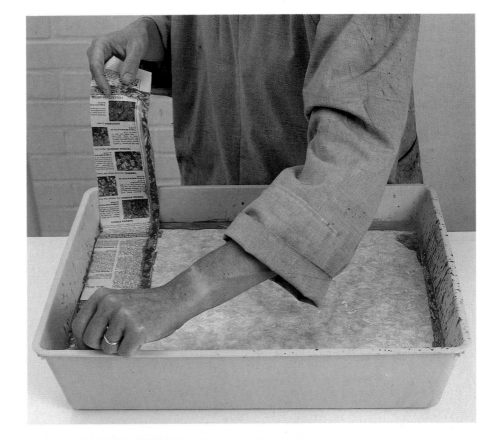

You will need paper strips to clean the surface of the tank. Any type of absorbent paper can be used – the more absorbent it is, the more quickly it will absorb any residual paint.

Anything can be used for a stylus as long as it is thin and fairly easy to pick up. Cocktail sticks can be particularly useful because they are disposable once the build-up of paint gets too heavy.

Basic Techniques

All marbling techniques work from the principle of spattering paints on to size, then swirling them with a stylus to make interesting patterns. Once mastered the technique is simple, but, like all new subjects, it may need some practice at first. The following pages will explain how to marble using carragheen moss and how to marble on fabric. There are also some useful ideas on experimenting with different patterns.

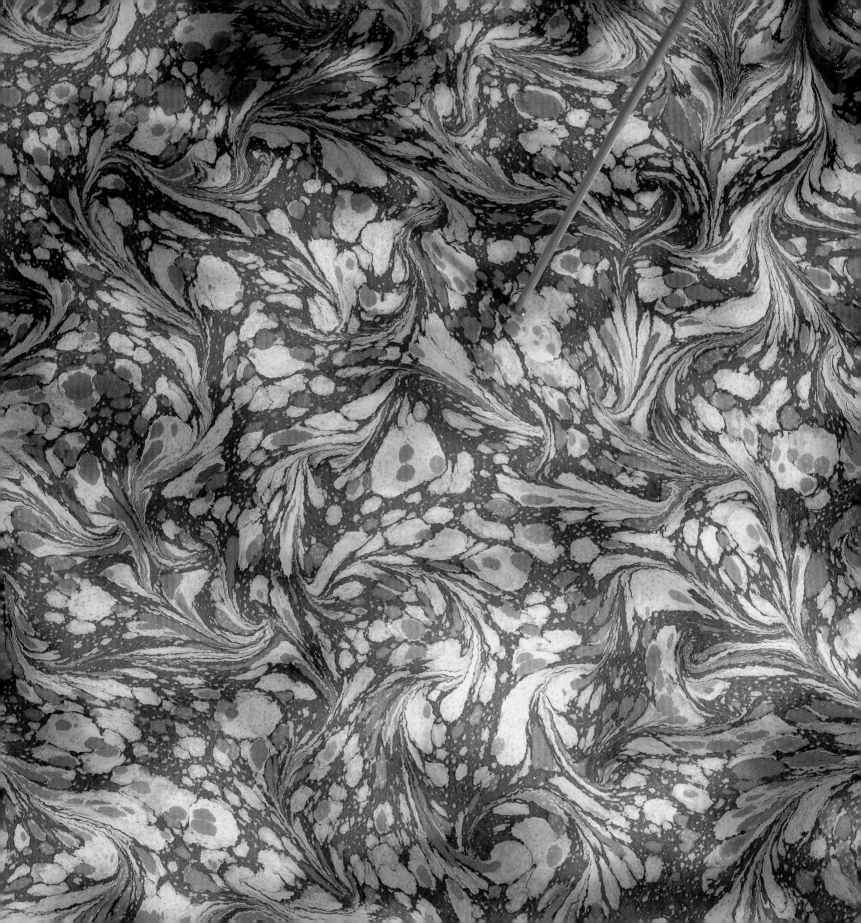

B asic techniques

THE ART OF MARBLING IS ACHIEVED BY FLOAT-ing paints on the surface of water or size (a mixture of water and gelatine) in a marbling tank. Beginners may find it easier to float the paints on water. However, using a thickened size with a stylus and different-sized combs will give you a wider variety of patterns.

Either oil- or water-based paints can be used. There's a lot to be said for starting off with water-based paints such as poster paints. They are cheaper, washable, and safe for small children. The only difference between oil- and water-based paints in terms of technique is that if you are using water-based paints you will have to sponge the paper with an alum solution first, to help the paints stick to the paper. Paper marbled with water-based paints must also be rinsed after being removed from the marbling tank. (The alum is important here, otherwise the paints will disappear along with the rinsing water!)

To make the alum solution, mix 60g (2oz) alum with 625ml (1 pint) of very hot water then stir until

It's very important to use a continuous movement when laying your paper on the surface of the size. Any hesitation at all may cause a watermark, as shown here.

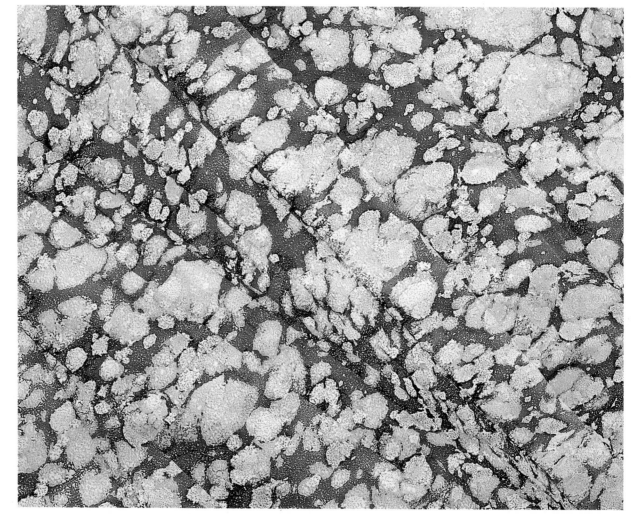

dissolved. As soon as the solution is cool enough it will be ready to use. If you decide to use water-based paints all the time, I suggest you set aside a container especially for making the solution.

Whichever paint you use, the first thing you must do is to prepare the size, or solution on which the paints are floated (see page 22).

PREPARING THE PAINTS

Once you have made the size, the next stage is to select and prepare your paints. Choose between two and four colours to begin with until you have mastered how to mix them. Squeeze approximately 2–3cm (1–1½in) paint into each of your separate pots, adding a little white spirit to each pot to thin the paint slightly – the paints should be runny but not too thin. Then add just a few drops of ox gall and mix well into the paints. Oil paints don't take kindly to being left standing overnight, so it's best to use them as soon as you have mixed them.

DISTRIBUTING THE PAINTS

After preparing your paints you must learn how to distribute them evenly on the size (see below). The secret here is to have just the right amount of paint on the brush to make the paint fall in a fine spray. If you have too much, the paint will fall in blobs and sink below the surface of the size instead. So remove as much paint as possible against the edge of the pot before beginning. It is best to practise flicking the paint with a firm but small flick of the wrist. You may find it easier at first to tap your brush against an old pencil or piece of wood to achieve the desired effect. That way you will be able to control the amount of paint on the size.

Like any other new subject, distributing the paint needs practice, so don't be discouraged if your first effort is less than perfect. As you become more skilled, you will learn to recognize problems as they arise. If the paint sinks, for example – and assuming this is not because you have applied too much – it is probably too thick and needs thinning

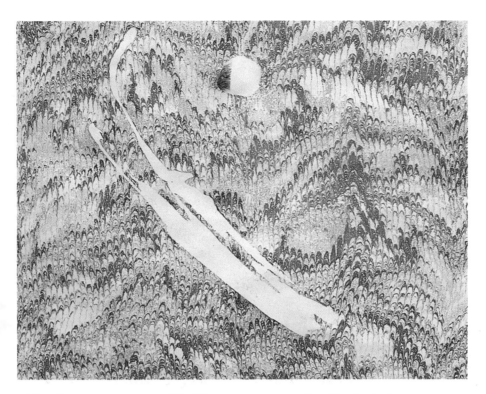

with a little more white spirit. The temperature of the size is also crucial. Paints will spread better if the size is at room temperature. If the size is too cold, the paints will contract. If, on the other hand, the paints spread too much they are either too thin or will have too much ox gall, although the odd blob of paint on the surface can be dispersed by blowing it gently. These and many other problems are covered more fully on page 32.

PATTERNS AND PRINTS

When you have distributed all the paints successfully on the size, you can then proceed to the real business of marbling: creating patterns by drawing a stylus or a knitting needle across the surface of the tank in a swirling motion. The final stage of the process is to make a print by laying your paper on the size, then leaving it to dry. You have now produced your first sheet of marbled paper!

The instructions on pages 22–25 are for oil marbling on cellulose size. For carragheen moss, see pages 26–27.

If, when laying paper on the surface of the size, air is trapped between the two, an air bubble, or blank patch, will appear on the paper as illustrated here. Always be sure to press the paper down carefully on the size to make sure the whole sheet makes contact with the paints.

▼ 1
MAKING THE SIZE

Fill the tank with cold water to a depth of 3–5cm (1½– 2in). Sprinkle a few tablespoonfuls of Courlose powder on the surface, stirring continuously until dissolved. The prepared size should be the consistency of very well diluted wallpaper paste and should move slightly when a stylus is drawn across it. (If necessary, add more powder.)

▼ 1
ADDING THE PAINTS

Take a strip of paper and draw it across the surface of the size to remove any particles of dust or paint. Stir each pot of paint with a brush and remove as much paint as possible against the edge of the pot. Flick your first colour on to the surface of the size so that the paint falls evenly over the surface in a fine spray.

2

*Continue adding the rest of the first colour with a flicking
action. This background colour should fully cover the
surface of the tank.*

3

*Add the rest of your colours with the same flicking action.
Don't pause between colours or surface tension in the size
will build up, and the paints will not spread properly.*

1

MARBLING (swirl pattern)
When all your colours are on the tank, slowly, but gently, swirl your paints across the tank with a stylus, thin knitting needle or cocktail stick. You can make either large free swirls or more formal, regular ones.

1

MAKING A PRINT
Holding a sheet of paper by two opposite corners, carefully lay one corner on the surface of the paint and continue to lay the rest of the sheet in one smooth action.

Without pausing, pick up the two corners nearest you and carefully lift the paper out of the marbling tank.

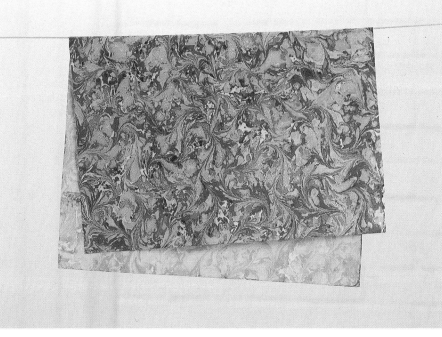

DRYING

Lay the marbled sheet on plastic sheeting or newspaper, or hang up with clothes pegs and leave to drip dry. When dry, press under weights.

Marbling on carragheen moss

CARRAGHEEN MOSS IS ANOTHER NAME FOR IRISH seaweed. It is available as a powder or dried leaf. Either can be used for marbling.

It is often mistakenly believed that oil marbling produces a grainy look on patterns, and that sharper, brighter colours can only be achieved with water-based paints. I believe the two illustrations below put that myth to rest. As you can see, it is the type of size that determines the sharpness of colours, not the type of paint.

Although carragheen moss creates better effects, however, it is more problematic than cellulose size. To begin with, it is not the most attractive substance. It looks like mud – and has a rather unpleasant smell, which grows stronger the longer it is left. It's also affected much more by temperature and can vary in thickness from batch to batch. An added disadvantage is that, unlike cellulose size, if you have to get rid of a batch you will have to start the whole lengthy process all over again, whereas

This is a perfect illustration of how different the same pattern and paints can look when applied on carragheen moss size and Courlose powder size. On the left-hand sheet, marbled on carragheen moss, the paint colours are much sharper, while the right-hand sheet, marbled on Courlose size, looks softer and more grainy.

with Courlose powder you can simply mix up a fresh tank.

As with Courlose powder size, temperature is vital. If the size gets too cold it will start to set. If you then have to thin it down you may make the size too loose to hold the pattern when combs are dragged across the tank. My advice is don't be squeamish – stir the size with your fingers. That way you will learn to feel the correct consistency and temperature. If the size is too thick, add a little warm water and stir well. I often find that size thickens overnight and needs thinning in the morning. Keep some size aside so that you can top up your tank if it evaporates or gets too thin. Once it begins to look murky and the paints no longer spread properly, you will know that it's time to make another batch. Bear in mind that any surplus can be frozen. Instructions for preparing carragheen moss are given below.

You will need:
- 1 saucepan
- approx. 30g (1oz) carragheen moss
- 15ml (1 tablespoon) borax (to prevent the carragheen moss from separating)
- Wooden spoon
- Muslin (or old nylon tights)
- Bowl

1
PREPARING CARRAGHEEN MOSS SIZE
Pour 2 litres (3¼ pints) water into a saucepan. Add the carragheen moss and the borax. Bring slowly to the boil, stirring occasionally with a wooden spoon, then simmer for about 4 minutes. Remove from the heat and add 1 litre (1½ pints) cold water. Leave to stand overnight.

2
Strain the size through a layer of muslin into a bowl. The size is now ready to use. Cover it to keep it clean – any dust on the surface will ruin your pattern.

Marbling on fabric

THE FREEDOM OF MOVEMENT IN MARBLED patterns lends itself particularly well to fabric. Although cotton and silk have been specified here, a wide range of other fabrics can also be used – even leather, although this will need varnishing afterwards for added protection. As when marbling on paper, the only materials to avoid are those with an artificial finish because they will not absorb the paints properly.

Before beginning to marble, it may be best to wash the fabric to remove any residue left after the manufacturing process. I would also recommend testing it for colour-fastness before using a large piece – silk, in particular, is expensive to waste.

As with marbling on paper, you can use oil- or water-based paints, although it's best to stick to oil paints on fabrics that will need a lot of washing,

1

LAYING THE FABRIC ON THE SIZE (method 1)
*With each person holding opposite sides of the square, dip the centre of the fabric in the tank. Both persons should then lay their side of the fabric down without hesitating, to avoid the possibility of a watermark (see page 20). Draw the fabric gently to the side edge of the tank and slide it out.
(Do not draw it towards you as when marbling paper.)
Immerse the fabric in a bowl containing 2.5 litres (4 pints) water and 5ml (1 teaspoon) vinegar, then hang the fabric up to dry.*

such as napkins, and use watercolours on materials that don't need as much day-to-day care. If in doubt, buy a paint produced specifically for fabrics, and follow the manufacturer's instructions. Alternatively, you can try any of the new fabric dyes now available.

The actual method of marbling on fabric is exactly the same as for marbling on paper. The only difference lies in the way you actually lay the fabric on the size. Fabric is trickier than paper, and you may have to resort to one of two methods as described below.

You will need:
- Squares of silk or cotton (pure cotton or a cotton-polyester mix)
- Extra pair of hands (or dowling and nails)
- Bowl or bucket of water
- 5ml (1 teaspoon) vinegar
- Iron
- Mild detergent
- Needle and thread

◀

LAYING THE FABRIC ON THE SIZE (method 2)
Nail the two sides of fabric to a narrow piece of wood or dowling of the same length as the fabric, and, holding one side in each hand, lay it down on the size. Remove the fabric, immerse in water and hang up to dry, as in method 1.

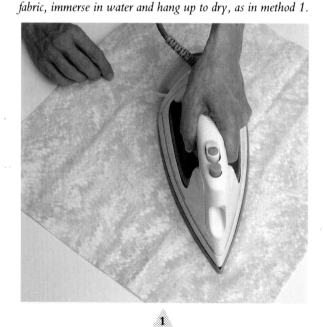

▲

SEALING
Once the fabric is dry, iron it on the reverse side to seal the paints, leave for a few days, then wash in mild soap, dry and iron once more. Trim the edges in case of thumb marks or crooked edges, then hem by machine or hand.

Experimenting with patterns

THE REAL PLEASURE OF MARBLING LIES IN THE unlimited patterns that can be created. Many of the most successful patterns are, however, traditional. All the ones described below are tried, tested and are easy to achieve, as long as you observe a few basic rules (see What Can Go Wrong, page 32).

All marbling patterns begin by spattering paint on to size. The paint is applied, one colour at a time, as described in the section on Basic Techniques (see page 21). Spattering usually acts as a basis on which to build another design, but sometimes it can be a pattern in itself, in which case you will have to take a little extra care over the finished result. You will also have to make decisions about how you want your pattern to look. Varying the size of the spatters, for example, can change the

1
SPATTER PATTERN
Spatter the first colour on to the size, taking care that the colour spreads out evenly to cover the surface. As you apply the second colour, spread it slightly less so that the spots hold their shape. The second colour will push out the first to form a vein.

emphasis of colours dramatically. Experiment until you achieve the desired effect.

SPATTERS, SWIRLS AND COMBS

For a spatter pattern to really work, you will need to use at least four colours. It doesn't matter which order you use them in but bear in mind that the pattern will look stronger if the darker colours go on first. In all patterns, the first colour to be applied will need a tiny amount of ox gall, and each successive colour slightly more.

Once you have mastered a spatter pattern, you can then progress to swirling the paints with a stylus or knitting needle. The most important thing to remember here is that when you lift the stylus out of the tank, you must be careful not to let any size on it drip on to your paper or your pattern will be spoilt. Use the stylus according to the effect you want: free sweeping movements for wild loose swirls or tiny regular ones for a more stylized look. Variations in size thickness will change your images a great deal – spatters and swirls will be much larger if your size is loose. Interesting results can also be achieved by spattering only three colours, swirling

2
Add the third and fourth colours in succession to make the pattern gain more depth.

them, then spattering a fourth colour on top.

Combed patterns add a different effect again, and it becomes more and more fascinating to watch how different the same colours can look when worked with different-sized combs. The smaller the comb the more intricate the pattern. This is seen to best effect in the Tiny Comb pattern, where the colours almost compete with the minute, intricate pattern to produce a very 'busy' look. (This is a particularly good pattern if you are using your marbled paper to cover small items.) If, however, you find the pattern too overwhelming with different colours, try using three or four tones of the same colour on tinted paper – the effect is stunning!

The range of patterns that can be achieved in marbling is infinite, and the beauty of the technique is that there are no hard-and-fast rules about how to use your colours. Dramatic contrasts can, for example, be achieved, by spattering the paints in separate bands of colours. When combed, the colours will then look separate and distinct, instead of all merging into one. And if you get bored with a particular look, you can always change it. Try, for example, using the same colours but simply reversing the order you apply them. You will be amazed at the difference it can make.

WHAT CAN GO WRONG
When trying a new technique for the first time, things are inevitably bound to go wrong. But as you become more skilled, and familiar with the problems that can arise, these mistakes will soon be corrected. One common mistake that many beginners make is to go on and on working over the colours they have floated. This is something you will learn in time. There is a limit to the amount of time paints can be left on the tank. If you mix them about too much, the pattern will just become a mess and individual colours indistinct. Other problems and their causes are given in the chart, right.

TROUBLESHOOTING

Problem	Cause
Colour drags when combed	Size is probably too thick. (Dilute with water). The paints may also be too thick. You may be using a comb that is too narrow. The tiny 3mm (⅛in) comb only works successfully on carragheen size. On Courlose powder size it may just drag the paint across the tank.
Colours sink	Paints are too thick, or there is too much paint on the brush.
Colour from previous sheet appears	Paint may have been applied in blobs which were too heavy and sank. (If this happens, the paint has a habit of re-emerging when you draw the comb or stylus through the size for the next pattern, and spoils the sheet.)
Paints not spreading properly	Paints are too thick. You may not have added enough ox gall, or may need to thin with white spirit. Size may be too cold, or the paints may be interacting badly (see below).
Paper prone to air bubbles	Paper is too dry.
Pattern distorts when combing	Teeth of the comb may be clogged up through constant use. A hair bristle or piece of fluff may have stuck to the comb.
Too much movement in the pattern	Size may be slightly too thin.
Pattern drags when comb or stylus is used	Size is too thick.

USING PAINT COLOURS CORRECTLY

All paints interact differently. The pigments in certain colours can actually stop the paints from spreading properly if they are applied in the wrong order. Others will positively encourage spreading. As a general rule, adding Lamp Black to dark colours, and Titanium White to light colours will help them spread. As you become more skilled, you will learn of other suitable combinations. Some well-spreading and badly-spreading paints are listed below. Paints that spread badly should not be avoided – just use them in combination with paints that spread too much.

Good spreaders (student oils): Flesh Pink, Paynes Grey, Lamp Black, Emerald Green, Titanium White, Indian Red, Cobalt Blue, Cerulean Blue, Cadmium Red, Yellow Ochre.

Bad spreaders (student oils): Flake White, Sap Green, Viridian, Crimson Lake, Burnt Sienna, Raw Umber.

◄ **1**

SWIRL PATTERN

Spatter four colours on to the surface of the tank as described on pages 30–31, then take a knitting needle or stylus and gently coax the paints into swirls, as desired.

Decorative Marbling

1
WIDE COMB PATTERN

*Create a spatter pattern as described on pages 30–31.
Then, using a stylus or knitting needle, draw the paint in
vertical lines up and down the tank in alternate opposite
directions, as when feathering a cake. Make sure you draw
the stylus right to the edge of the tank, otherwise the pattern
won't be distinct right to the edge.*

2
*Using a 12mm (½in) comb, draw the comb slowly across
the tank in the opposite direction from the feathering.*

3

Work the pattern further by repeating the feathering after combing. Take care to make the last feathering even and, again, right to the edge.

Decorative Marbling

TINY COMB PATTERN

*Follow the instructions for Step 1 of the Wide Comb
pattern, using a stylus or knitting needle.*

2

*Follow the instructions for step 2 of the Wide Comb
pattern, using a tiny 3mm (⅛in) comb instead of a wide
12mm (½in) one.*

3

*Draw your stylus or knitting needle across the tank in a
'snake-like' movement as shown.*

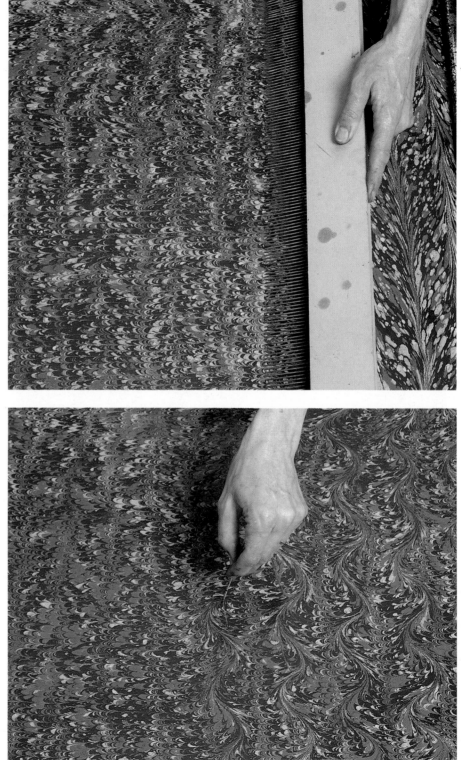

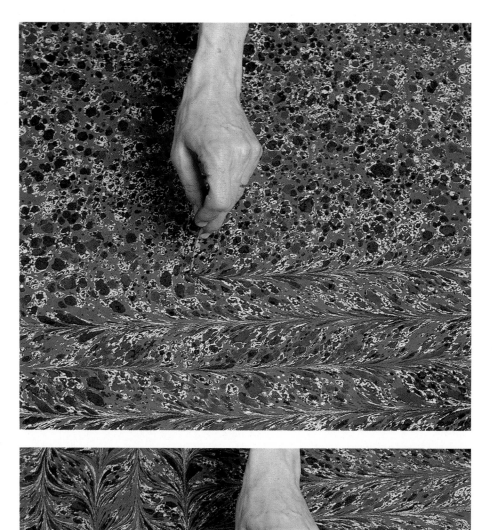

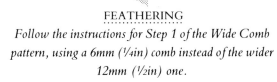

1
FEATHERING

Follow the instructions for Step 1 of the Wide Comb pattern, using a 6mm (¼in) comb instead of the wider 12mm (½in) one.

2

Draw your stylus or knitting needle at right angles to the first lines. As you lift the stylus out of the tank, be very careful not to let a drop of size on it drip on to the pattern and spoil it.

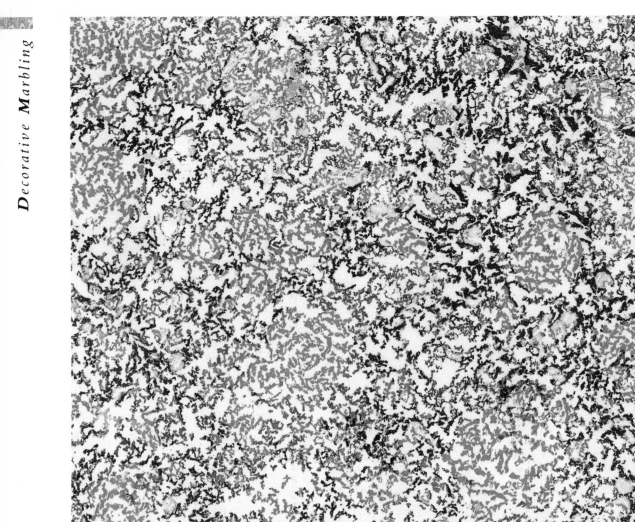

LACE PATTERN

*Curious and interesting random patterns can be produced by
leaving paints on the tank for differing periods of time. The
illustration above shows the pattern produced after
spattering four colours on to the tank and leaving them for
more than three hours.*

CLOUD IMAGE

A second print can be taken from the residue of a preceding pattern. Instead of cleaning off the surface of the size after you have taken the first print, swirl the paint in from the edges so that it covers the size once again. Lay down the sheet of paper as before. The strength of the image depends on the amount of paint remaining from the first sheet.

Projects

You can put your marbled paper and fabric to countless uses, and have lots of fun in the process. The projects that follow include a wide range of ideas, from transforming an old tray into an attractive gift to making a stunning silk scarf – and a beautiful pleated lampshade for your home. But, don't forget, these are only suggestions. With just a little imagination, the possibilities are, literally, endless!

Giftwrapping paper

This first project is an obvious one to start with. It is simple to do, and very satisfying. Children have an instant use for their creation, and even the tiniest of token presents is enhanced by uniquely designed paper. For an attractive finishing touch, choose ribbon or string to complement one of the colours in your paper.

As with any type of marbling, you must make sure you use the right type of paper (see page 17). The best choice is either tinted or textured papers used with gold or silver paint. Although expensive, these paints are very effective for marbling. Use them in exactly the same way as oil paints, adding white spirit and ox gall to thin them down. Their spreading ability can vary a great deal, however, and you may have to add a neutral colour to the silver or gold to 'hold' it. For example, if you are marbling a sheet with green and gold in it, then mix a tiny amount of your green mixture to the gold, and the gold will then have a bit more body.

Try, when laying the sheet on the size, not to let the edges dip into the tank too much. Otherwise you will end up with size and paint trickling across the back of the paper.

You will need:
A choice of:
- Kraft paper *or*
- Textured paper *or*
- Tinted paper

- Gold or silver paints
- Ribbon (optional)

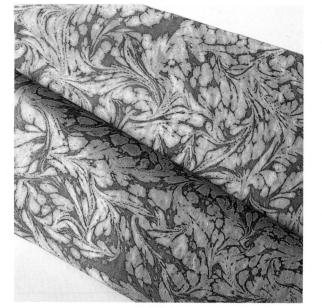

Papers marbled with gold paint

A selection of marbled giftwrapping papers

Pencil tub and pencils

These marbled pencils and matching tub make attractive desk accessories. You can use plain or painted pencils; if plain, you can paint the end of them to match the paper. The instructions below are for round pencils, as they are easier to cover than straight-sided ones.

You will need:
- Cylindrical tub
- Paint (enamel- or oil-based)
- Brush
- Measuring tape
- Ruler
- Cutting blade
- Marbled paper
- Round pencils
- Glue
- Rag
- Varnish (matt or gloss)

Making the pencil tub

1 Making sure that the container is thoroughly clean and dry, paint the top edge, base and, if necessary, the inside, in a colour which complements the marbled paper you plan to use. Then measure the exact dimension of the tub, allowing 3mm (⅛in) overlap where the seam joins, and cut out one piece of marbled paper to this size.

2 Glue the unmarbled side of the paper on to the tub and press in place evenly. Rub all over with a rag to smooth out any air bubbles.

Making the pencils

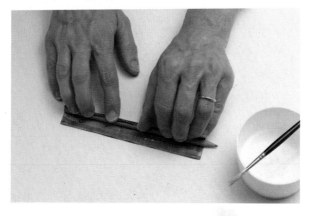

Measure the diameter of the pencil, adding 3mm (⅛in) for overlap, then measure the length of the pencil up to the base of the sharpened end. Cut out a piece of paper this size and spread glue over the unmarbled side. Holding the edge of the paper, firmly roll the pencil over the glue and smooth out any air bubbles with a rag. Sharpen the pencil to neaten the top edge.

Greetings cards

Marbled patterns on different weights of paper and card can be used to make attractive personalized cards and gift tags. The techniques for marbling on card are the same as for paper, but card is less malleable so you must be careful to lay it on the tank with exactly the right amount of pressure. You may find it easier to mount your marbled paper on card rather than marbling directly on the card itself. Three ideas are given below.

You will need:
- Ruler
  A choice of:
- 1 sheet of marbled paper and plain card (postcard weight) *or* Marbled card

- Cutting blade
- Tracing paper
- Newspaper
- Gold felt tip pen
- Hole punch (optional)
- Ribbon for gift tags (optional)
- Glue

Making marbled letters

This is a particularly amusing idea for young children. Glue the marbled paper on to fairly stiff card and leave to dry, or take a piece of marbled card. From a newspaper, trace the letters of your message on to the marbled side of the paper. Using a cutting blade, very carefully cut out the letters individually, taking care that the blade doesn't slip. Once the letters are cut out, you can give them to a child and let him/her put them together.

Making a card

Putting a marbled frame on a picture

Make gift tags to match your cards by folding marbled card in half, punching a hole in the corner and inserting some ribbon.

(Use marbled card or marbled paper glued to card.) Trim the marbled card to the size required, fold it in half firmly, then open it out flat. Cut a window out of the front and edge it with gold pen. Write a message inside the frame.

Take a piece of marbled paper the size of the print or photograph you will use. Cut out a window to make a frame. Fold a piece of plain card in half. Glue the picture to the front and leave to dry, then glue the marbled frame over the top.

*C*ard envelope and stationery

Edwardian ladies often used pretty card envelopes to keep their letters in. A marbled card envelope is easy to make and is useful for storing not only special letters, but photographs, handkerchiefs or stationery. Use pretty tinted papers for your letters, or make your own marbled stationery, taking care to make the marbling pale and light so that you will be able to read any writing on the paper. Simply create a cloud image as described on page 39 and keep the paints delicate by putting much less on the size than normal. Alternatively, you could always mask off a portion of the paper and just marble a border.

The instructions below are for an A5-sized envelope and A5 stationery. (You could also use A4 paper for the latter, but it will have to be folded.) The envelope can be made of marbled card or a sheet of marbled paper firmly glued to light card.

You will need:
A choice of:
- Marbled card *or*
- Sheet of marbled paper glued to card

- A5 envelope (for template)
- Pencil
- Scissors
- Cutting blade
- Length of ribbon 50cm (20in) long
- Glue
- A5 or A4 sheets of marbled paper (for stationery)

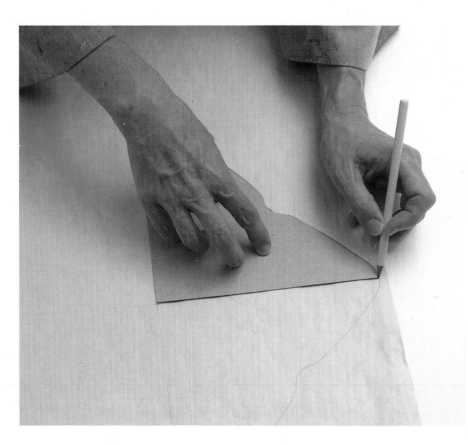

1 Unglue an A5 envelope and, with a pencil, trace around the shape on the back of your marbled card or paper.

2 Carefully cut around the outline of the opened-out envelope with a pair of scissors.

3 Using your cutting blade, cut two slits, 2.5cm (1in) apart by 2.5cm (1in) long, in the middle of the card or paper for the ribbon.

4 Take the ribbon and thread it through the two slits which you have cut on the paper, with the two ribbon ends on the marbled side of the card. Following the creases on your template, fold and glue the three flaps into position.

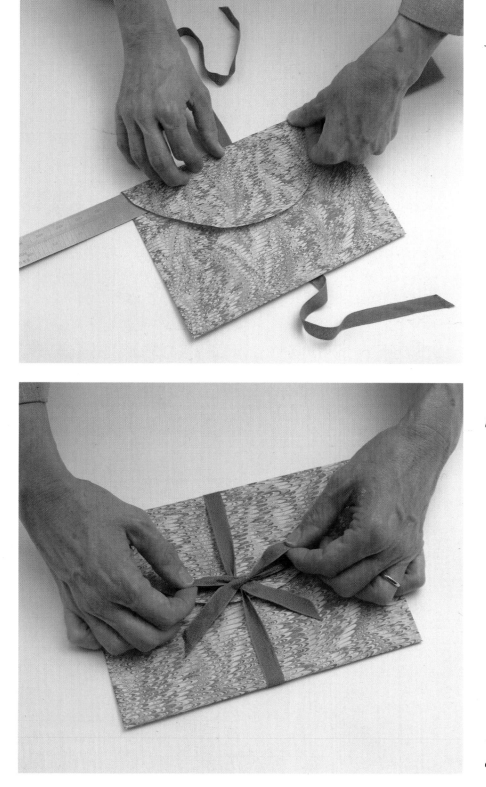

5 *Crease the final flap of the envelope firmly and fold it into shape.*

6 *Wrap the ribbon around the envelope and tie a bow above the flap to finish.*

The completed card envelope with stationery.

Decorative tray

Pretty marbled paper can transform an ordinary tray into something really special. As an extra finishing touch, a piece of felt or baize can be added to the back.

You will need:
- Plain wooden tray
- Gloss or satin paint and paint brush
- 1 sheet of marbled paper fractionally larger than the inside of the tray
- Cutting blade
- Glue
- Heat-resistant varnish (gloss or matt)

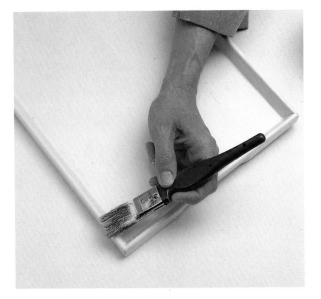

1 Making sure that the sides of the tray are clean, paint the edges and handles in whatever colour you choose, to match the paper. Leave to dry.

2 Paste the sheet of marbled paper with glue on the unmarbled side and lay it on the tray, marbled side up, smoothing it down well to remove any air bubbles. Leave for about 30 minutes until the glue has dried.

3 When the glue has dried completely, apply three coats of heat-resistant varnish (gloss or matt) to the base and sides of the tray.

Picture frame

Marbled paper has become very popular for use in picture framing, either with a mount entirely covered with marbled paper or a tiny band of marbling on a plain mount. (You could also buy a ready-made mount.)

You will need:

A choice of:

- Ready-made mount *or*
- Card (approximately 3mm (⅛in) thick and measuring 20 × 10cm (8 × 4in))

- Sheet of marbled paper
- Cutting blade
- Glue
- Ruler and pencil
- Tinted paper
- Gold or silver felt tip pen

Making your own mount

1 Take the card and cut out a square, rectangle or circle with the cutting blade. Glue a piece of marbled paper over the entire mount, including the window. For square or rectangular mounts, draw a diagonal line approximately 5cm (2in) from the corner. Repeat on the other three corners. Join the tips of the lines to make a square or rectangle.

2 Cut out the rectangle and slit each of the four diagonal lines to make four flaps. Fold back the flaps and glue on the unmarbled side. Fold back and press down.

Making a mount with a marbled trimming

Buy a ready-made mount. Otherwise, using card as before, cover this time with plain paper, preferably tinted. Cut the window to the required size 6mm (¼in) in from the window and draw a gold line around it. Draw a further gold line 12mm (½in) outside the first. This forms a border within which to lay the strips of marbled paper. Cut two 6mm (¼in) strips of marbled paper for top and bottom. Cut a further two of the same size for the sides. Lay these evenly between the two lines. Before gluing, cut the corners of the marbled paper at a diagonal angle so that they fit together very neatly, bearing in mind also that the pattern of the marbled paper must match the top and sides. Glue the marbled paper and lay accurately along the pencil line, making sure that the strips are straight.

Hat box

Three identical sheets of marbled paper have been used for this hat box. In the pattern below, we are using a box 40cm (16in) in diameter and 25cm (10in) deep. Of course, you can use the same instructions for any round box and reduce or increase the marbled paper accordingly. If you wish to cover the base of the box, I recommend using kraft paper or any other plain paper and cutting another circle the same size as the one for the lid.

You will need:
- Round ready-made box, 40cm (16in) in diameter and 25cm (10in) deep
- Pencil
- Marbled paper
- Scissors
- Cutting blade
- Glue and a 2.5cm (1in) brush
- Felt tip pen, or emulsion paint to match the paper
- Hole punch
- Wide ribbon or cord of suitable length

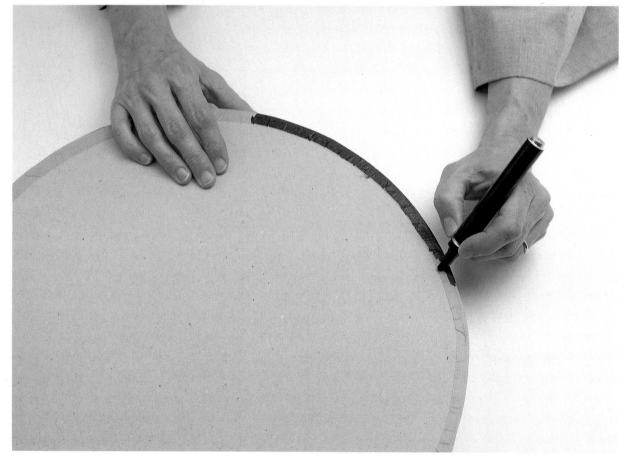

1 Using the box lid as your template, draw around the outline of the box on the unmarbled side of the paper and cut a circle 6mm (¼in) smaller all round than the pencilled drawing. Cut three pieces of marbled paper, 44 × 27.5cm (17½ × 11in), followed by three measuring 44 × 6.5cm (17½ × 2½in). (The latter are for the rim of the lid.) Before gluing paper in position, paint edge of lid with emulsion paint, overlapping top and rim by about 12mm (½in). Repeat on rim of base of box. Your disc of paper on the box should cover the paint, leaving about 3mm (⅛in) paint showing. Leave paint to dry.

2 Glue the marbled paper disc for the hat box lid on the unmarbled side. This must be positioned carefully so that an equal amount of coloured edging shows all the way round. Press down firmly in position, smoothing out the paper from the centre.

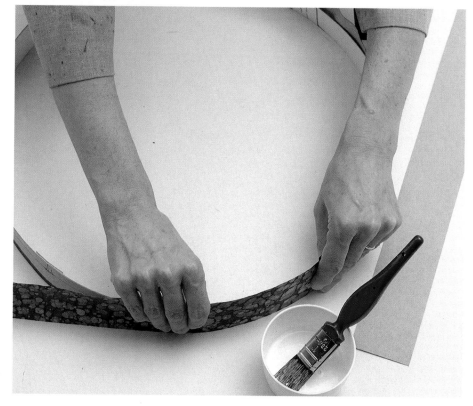

3 Glue the first piece of paper for the rim of the lid (measuring 44 × 6.5cm (17½in × 2½in)) and, beginning at a seam in the lid, position the paper so that 3mm (⅛in) paint is left showing, to balance the top of the lid. Repeat with the next two pieces of marbled paper, allowing a small overlap.

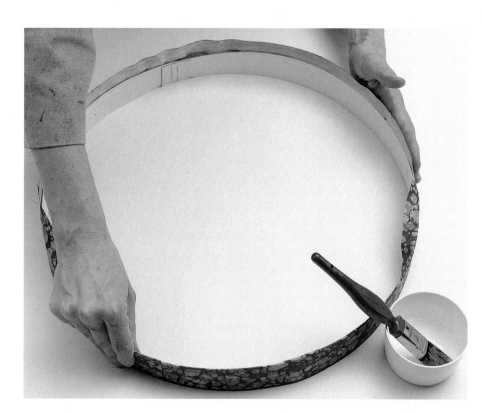

4 Using a brush, reglue the exposed pieces of marbled paper on the wrong side, then glue the inside of the rim. Repeat for the sides of the base, being careful to smooth each panel well before applying the next. Turn over the top edge after applying more glue, as with the lid.

5 To attach ribbon, punch two holes on opposite sides of the box. Take a length of ribbon and insert ends into eyelet holes, tying knots on the side. Alternatively, cut two pieces of ribbon and tie a generous bow centred above the lid.

The completed hat box.

Candleshade

At the turn of the century, candles were still a major source of lighting, and were often adorned by charming shades which shed a gently diffused light. The fashion for candleshades has recently revived and marbled paper makes an excellent material. Choose your paper according to where you want the light to fall. Pale marbled paper will let some of the light glow through the shade, while darker paper will diffuse the light up and down.

A word of warning when making candleshades. It is obviously essential to make sure the flame does not come in contact with the paper. Bear in mind that the shade rests on a brass follower which, as the candle burns, will slowly glide down the candle, carrying the candleshade with it. It is therefore very important that the shade fits the follower exactly. The best way to ensure this is to measure the shade carefully so that it fits the follower exactly, and then double check by holding the two upside down. If your measurements are right, the shade should stay fixed to the follower. All commercially produced followers carry instructions and warnings, with advice about which type of candle to use. The shades below can also be used on electric candle bulbs – in which case, you will need to buy a brass electric adaptor to hold the shade over the bulb.

The instructions which follow are for a 10cm (4in) candleshade, which is an ideal size for use with either candles or bulbs.

You will need:
- Tracing paper
A choice of:
- Marbled card *or*
- Marbled paper ironed on to bonding card *or*
- Marbled paper bonded on to card with spray adhesive
- Pencil
- Cutting blade
- Felt tip pen
- Masking tape
- Brass follower
- Glue
- Clothes pegs

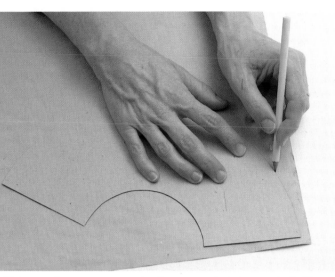

1 Using tracing paper, trace the diagram, which is exactly half size. Carefully repeat the right hand half by turning the pattern over. Do not repeat the seam allowance. Transfer the pattern to any one of the following: (a) marbled card, (b) marbled paper which has been ironed on to a proprietary brand of bonding card, or (c) marbled paper bonded on to card with spray adhesive. Draw around the template of your chosen alternative and cut out the shape.

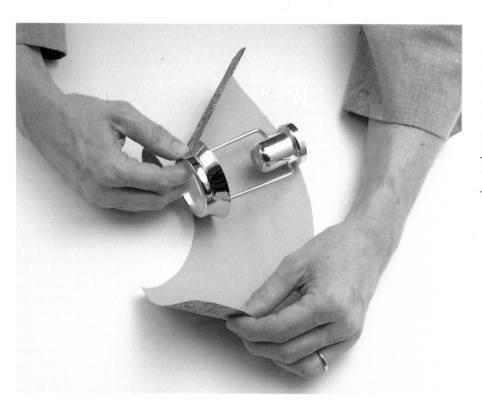

2 *Using a colour of your choice, use a felt tip pen to edge both the top and bottom of the shade. Join the side edges of the shade together with masking tape and try the shade on the follower to make absolutely sure that the shade is firmly fixed on to it.*

3 *Stick the sides of the shade together, gluing the overlap under its corresponding edge. Hold it in place with two clothes pegs until dry.*

The completed candleshade.

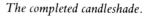

*P*leated lampshade

This stylish lampshade is surprisingly easy to make and would look lovely in any room. The instructions are for making a 25cm (10in) lampshade, which is suitable for a lampbase 30–50cm (12–20in) high.

You will need:
- 2 sheets of 50 × 63cm (20 × 25in) marbled paper, as closely matching in pattern as possible
- Cutting blade
- Glue
- 2 rulers
- Hole punch
- 1m (3ft) length of 2.5cm (1in) wide ribbon
- 1m (3ft) length of 5mm (¼in) wide ribbon
- Lamp frame
- Upholstery needle

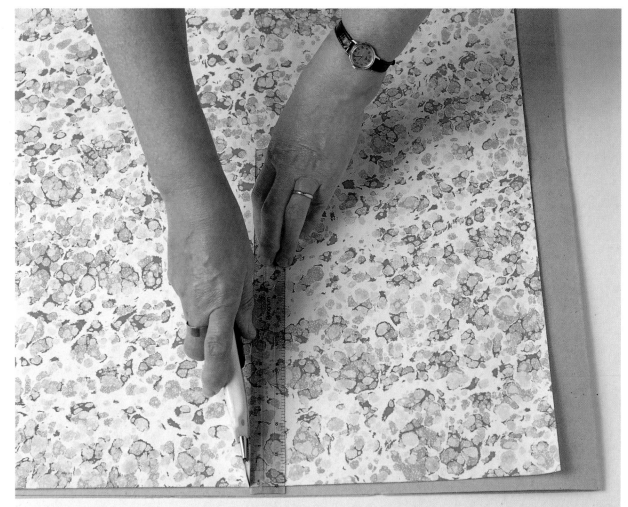

1 Take the two sheets of marbled paper and cut them in half lengthways, using a cutting blade to produce a sharp edge. You will now have four pieces of paper, each measuring 25 × 63cm (10 × 25in).

2 Using two rulers, pleat each sheet of paper to make concertina folds. To do this, fold the paper over one ruler, then fold it back over the other.

3 Apply glue along the underside end pleats of two sheets, and then on the marbled side of the other two. Glue the edges together to make one long sheet.

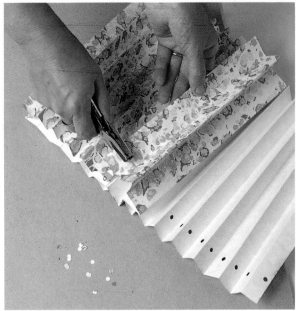

4 Mark 2.5cm (1in) from the top of the pleats, then punch a hole through each pleat using the hole punch. Ensure that all the holes align. You should be able to punch through several layers of pleats at once.

5 Thread the wider piece of ribbon through the punched holes so that you have two ends coming through at the front.

6 Lay the shade down with the frame on top. Secure them together using the upholstery needle and thin ribbon. Turn the frame over and arrange the pleats so that they are evenly distributed around the frame.

The completed lampshade.

Patchwork screen

I love screens, particularly those covered with cut-out scraps dating from Victorian times. Inspired by a marbled screen made by the painter Katherine Church – and by the delightful effect achieved by my husband when he wallpapered our bathroom in a patchwork of 12.5cm (5in) squares – I thought it would be fun to include a marbled 'patchwork' screen here. This is ideal for beginners, who will not yet be producing large sheets of marbled paper.

It's a good idea to work out approximately how you want the panels to look before you begin. In this case the front and back of the screen look different, but you can make them the same if you prefer. The first side is made up of a series of 10cm (4in) squares using one pattern of marbled paper to unify the design. It's probably best to make this 'base' pattern a fairly dark colour. It then won't matter how bright the alternate squares are, or how many different patterns you use. Just like a patchwork quilt, in fact!

You will need:
- Ready-made screen
- Steel ruler and pencil
- Squares and sheets of marbled paper
- Glue
- Cutting blade
- Trimming for top and sides of screen
- Scissors
- Matt varnish (optional)

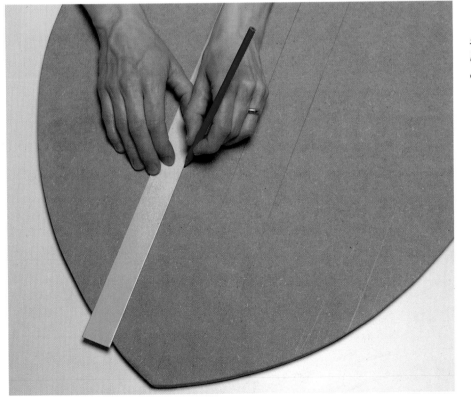

1 Draw a centre line from top to bottom of the screen. Draw two further lines 5cm (2in) on either side of the centre line.

2 Put your squares of marbled paper on the ground and work out the pattern you require, matching the squares up accordingly.

3 Begin by gluing the first square centre top. This is your guide. You should work three or four squares down the centre and then fill in either side. Complete each panel in the same manner.

4 With a cutting blade at right angles to the edge of the screen, trim over-hanging patches.

5 Now for the back of the panel. Follow the same basic principle, using larger pieces marbled in the same colour. I have chosen a very loose size with a swirled pattern so that the appearance is much more random than on the front of the screen. Trim off excess patches as for front of screen.

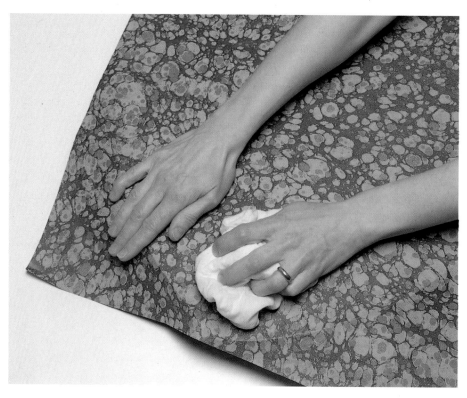

6 To finish off, choose a trimming to go around the edge, preferably in a dark colour which won't show marks. Apply the glue and press the trimming up the sides and along the top of the screen, stretching it slightly as you go along and pressing down well. Finally, the screen can be given a matt coat of varnish for protection, or sprayed with a proprietary brand of dirt repellant.

The completed screen.

Table mat and coasters

The table mat and coasters below will grace any table. Make them in matching or complementary colours. The instructions below are for straight-sided mats, since these are obviously much easier to cut out than round ones. You can, if you wish, cover the mat entirely with marbled paper, but there is a lot to be said for mounting a piece of marbled paper on card and painting a border around it, as described on page 74. It will protect the edges of the marbled paper from getting scuffed with time and use. To make the coasters, follow the instructions for the mat, using smaller pieces of card as required.

You will need:
- Marbled paper
- One piece of card, measuring 20 × 25cm (8 × 9in) (for the mat), plus required number of pieces of card measuring 11.5 × 8.5cm (4½ × 3½in) (for coasters)
- Pencil and ruler
- Paint
- Paint brush
- Cutting blade
- Glue
- Heat-resistant varnish

Covering the mat with marbled paper

1 Edge the mat with gold paint. Use a ruler to make sure the line is completely straight and an even distance from the edge all round.

2 Using a cutting blade, cut a piece of marbled paper just fractionally smaller all around than the size of the mat.

3 Glue the paper on the unmarbled side and press it down smoothly to remove any wrinkles or air bubbles. When the glue has dried, varnish the top and sides with two coats of varnish, checking to make sure that none of the brush bristles are left on the varnish.

Using a border

1 First, decide how wide the border is going to be. Using a pencil and ruler, draw a border 2.5cm (1in) wide around the inside edges of the card. Using an undercoat if necessary, paint the whole border in a colour which complements your marbled paper. Leave to dry.

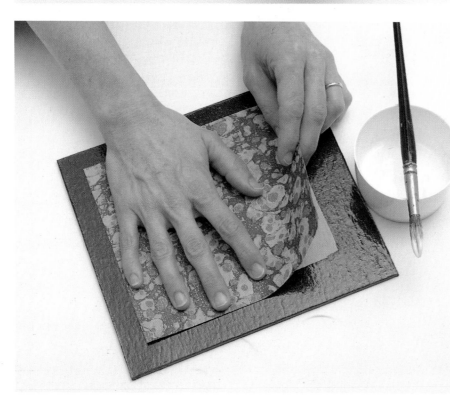

2 Meanwhile, cut the marbled paper into one piece measuring 18 × 20.5cm (7¼ × 8¼in) and glue the unmarbled side. Place the paper on the mat, being careful to get it absolutely straight. When the glue has dried, varnish the top and sides with two coats of varnish, checking to make sure that none of the brush bristles are left on the varnish.

The completed table mats and coaster.

Silk scarf

A pretty silk scarf offers the perfect opportunity for trying out your marbling skills on fabric. Once you have marbled and treated the silk (see page 28), most of the work is done, though bear in mind that silk is quite a tricky fabric to sew. Use good-quality steel pins or basting stitches, as described below.

You will need:
- Square of marbled silk
- Extra equipment for marbling on fabric (see pages 28–29)
- Needle and thread
- Pins
- Iron

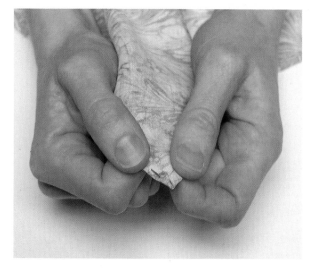

1 Turn in all four raw edges of the silk, following the illustration above for the corners, and press. Turn in again and fix the hem in place, using pins or basting stitches.

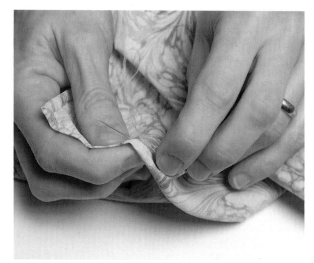

2 Hem the fabric by hand with small neat stitches and using a fine needle and thread. Alternatively, use a sewing machine with a straight or zigzag stitch.

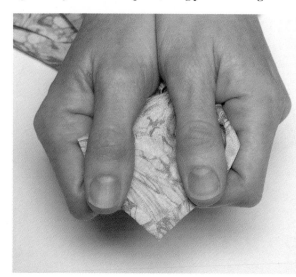

3 Remove the pins or basting stitches, and press with a cool iron to leave a neat crisp edge.

List of suppliers

Screens
The Dormy House
Dept CL
Stirling Park
East Portway Ind Est
Andover
Hampshire SP10 3TZ
24 hr tel 0264 365808

Screen Scene
The Garden House
Mountstephen
Uffculme
Devon EX15 3BX
Tel 0884 841044

Brass holders
Compton Marbling
Lower Lawn Barns
Tisbury
Salisbury
Wiltshire SP3 6SG
Tel 0747 871 147

Or any retailer selling candle lighting

Hat box
40cm (16in) diameter only in cardboard from
Compton Marbling

Bonding card
Any shop selling lampshade-making equipment

Carragheen moss
Ox gall
Falkiner Fine Papers
76 Southampton Row
London WC1B 4AR
Tel 071–831 1151

Or any specialist craft shop, for example, Dryad
or from Compton Marbling

Courlose powder
Compton Marbling

Alum powder
Falkiner Fine Papers
Or any specialist craft shop, for example, Dryad

Borax
Most chemists

Wire frame for lampshade
Frames for 10cm (4in), 12.5cm (5in), 17.5cm (7in),
21cm (8½in) and 25–30cm (10–12in) all available
from Compton Marbling
Otherwise as for bonding card

Index

Acknowledgements

I would like to thank the following people for their help and encouragement: Yvonne Kellock, Chris Newton, David Burnett, Jon Bouchier and in particular Chris Wallis (Compton Marbling) and Miren Lopategui (editor).

I would also like to thank my husband, Humphrey, and daughter, Angelica Cotterell, for their enormous and invaluable support.